For a Limited Time Only

"Those who use well what they are given, even more
will be given, and they will have an abundance."
– Matthew 25:29 (NLT)

Dedication

Joanna and I dedicate this book to our beautiful children, and the generations that come after us. May the Lord be gracious to you, and may you run your race well.

We love you, and we have prayed for you!

Acknowledgments

There are many people that I would like to thank. People who have specifically shaped my life greatly, and as a result, had a major influence on this book.

First, to my beautiful wife, Joanna. Honey you are my favorite person, and best friend. Your strength and loyalty are just what I needed. I am so thankful God placed you by my side, and I am so excited to walk out a lifetime together with you. You are the best and I love you.

To my parents. I couldn't be more thankful to have such amazing and supportive parents. You are an unending source of strength and stability for me, and I could not have become the man I am today without you. Until the end, I love you.

To all the former, and current leadership of TCI. Together you have built the spiritual house that has shaped my Christian walk. Wherever I go, and whatever I do, the DNA of prayer, missions, the Word of God, integrity, and the desire for His presence will go with me. Thank you!

To Jonathan Cook. I am forever indebted to you for taking me under your wing when I was 20 years old. Oh the doors that have opened for me as a result of you putting your loving and strong arms around me- you know I love you, thank you.

To Dr. Bob Abramson. This project could not have become a reality without you. You have always been there to help me, never desiring anything in return, just to simply see me succeed. Thank you for your time, effort, faith, words of encouragement, and most importantly, thank you for your love. You have made a difference in me.

Contents

Cover design by McCall Cox through Radiant Printing
Edited by Daniel Marino

You may contact Pastor Grittner through
www.golifespring.church

Introduction

It was a cool summer's day in Africa. An old wise man was sitting on a wooden bench overlooking a beautiful lake. Suddenly, a young preacher came and sat down next to the old wise man. The young minister was contemplating getting the most out of his life so he began to prod the older man for answers. After a few minutes of questioning, the old wise man had his own set of questions. "How old are you, David?" The young man replied, "41." The old man leaned back, laughed and said, "Ah, David, you have so much time left to do all that God has put in your heart." But before David could enjoy the words that the old man just shared, the wise man violently stuck his 70-year-old, bony finger right in David's face and said, "But you don't have nearly as much time as you think you have."

I first heard this story at a pastoral staff meeting. The person recounting the story was the senior pastor of the Church, Tom Peters. Pastor Tom was sharing the accounts of the conversation to a few younger ministers who were eager to change the world. At the time, I was the youngest person in the room. After we all had a good laugh at David's encounter with such a sobering thought, Pastor Tom looked at me and asked, "How old are you Dan?" To which I replied, "Well, Pastor, I'm 30! Still young and vibrant" (yes, I actually said that). Pastor Tom leaned back and laughed and said…. "Dan, you've got your whole life in front of you. You can do all that God has put in your heart." Then he wagged his finger at me and said, "But you don't have nearly as much time as you think you have!"

Today is most likely a good day for you. You find yourself reading this book. You may be in your car, at your house, in a coffee shop, at your desk, or in your favorite chair. You could be outside working, but instead you find yourself being able to relax and read. Ah, yes, this is a good day for you. You have so much time to do what God has put in your heart. But you don't have nearly as much time as you think you have!

My mom had three boys. All of us were involved with sports year round. It took a lot of money to raise us, and my parents didn't always have a lot of extra money because we were involved in many extracurricular activities.

One spring evening my mom and I went to Walmart to buy some new sporting equipment for the upcoming baseball season. When we were in line to pay for my new equipment, I saw a big pink package of bubble gum. I begged my mom to simply add it to my equipment tab. She wasn't going to buy it. And somehow, even at my naïve age, I thought the price of all my equipment had something to do with it. So, I conveniently suggested, "Mom just put it on the credit card!"

Credit cards are used so that people can buy things they can't afford. Generations before us didn't believe in buying things on credit. They said things like, "If I don't have the money to pay for it, then I won't buy it." Generations later, people are buying so many things that they can't afford, and the credit cards help them do this. In other words, the credit card allows you to stretch your hand and grab what isn't yours.

Your time is not a credit card; you can't just make more time. Your time is like a stack of dollar bills: every day you have to hand over 24, every week 168 and every year 8,760 hours. Time, instead, is like the precious gold found deep within the earth's surface. It's like the beautiful red rubies and crystal clear diamonds found in the hills of Africa.

The Bible says that our life is like a vapor; we are here today and yet gone tomorrow. Some people say that time is money, but I say that it is so much more: because you can always make more money, but you can never ever make more time. Time is priceless because you are here for a limited time only.

Chapter 1: Time Charts

Have you ever tried to figure out how many hours you have left to live? I know it's a weird question, and one that no one has the answer to, but I have a formula that can help you understand how much time you have left! The Huffington post reported that the average life span for an American is 78 years old.[1]

For a frame work let's just say that your passing from this earthly life into eternity will not be at 78 years of age, like the average person, but that the Lord will grant you 7 more years, until 85 years old. Again, no one knows the day or the hour that they will pass from this life to the other. However, I think that most people see themselves living a long life, having grandchildren, etc. So with that being said, let's see how much time you have left to live.

Obviously there are 24 hours in a day and 365 days in a year. If you multiply 24 (hours in a day)

---

[1] "U.S. Life Expectancy Ranks 26th In The World, OECD Report Shows," Huffington Post.

by 365 (days in a year) that means there are 8,760 hours in a year. Every person on this earth, no matter their skin color or economic status, size or weight, all have 8,760 hours in a year. I'd now like to introduce you to something that I call "The Lifetime Equation."

"The Lifetime Equation"
85 (age of death) - Your current age = Years left to live x 8,760 (hours in a year) = Hours left to live

With this equation, one can get an estimate as to how many hours they have left to live. For example, if you are 85 years old when you die and you are currently 25 years old, you have 60 years left to live. So if you take 60 (years left to live) times 8,760 (hours in a year) you have 525,600 hours left to live.

Imagine if you were 25 years old, and that was all the money you had left to live on for the rest of your life. Would that change the way you spent your money? Similarly, if you are 40, in relation to our equation, you have 394,200 hours left, and if you are 60 years old you have 219,000 hours left to live.

Let's stop there! I understand how this formula can quickly become depressing. The point that I am making is that time is quickly passing you by, and you don't have as much time as you think you have. If you haven't already, find out how many hours you have left specifically. Plug your information into the Lifetime Equation this way… 85 (age of death) – (your current age) _____ = _____ (that's how many years you have left to live). Now take that number, and multiply it by 8,760 (hours in a year) = _____ (amount of hours you have left to live, if you die at the age of 85).

I once asked a middle school boy how many hours he has left to live. He confidently responded with the statement, "Oh, I don't know, probably a couple billion." After we plugged his Lifetime Equation in, he found out he had much less than that.

I am so glad that you are reading this book. Because if you're not careful, you can live your whole life not being aware of the brevity of life. In doing so, your life becomes that of a Groundhog Day: monotonous, mundane and repetitive. WAKE UP!! God has something for you to do specifically. Do you know what it is?

Matthew 25

The Bible actually shares that it is a sin to waste your life. You might think, what do you mean, it's a sin to waste my life? You might be thinking that the life you have is yours to live the way you want. Please consider this parable that

Jesus Christ shared in the 25th chapter of the Gospel of Matthew, verses 14-29. It is important that you read this passage to comprehension, as it is central to the theme of the book.

Matthew 25:14-29 (NLT)

"Again, the Kingdom of Heaven can be illustrated by the story of a man going on a long trip. He called together his servants and entrusted his money to them while he was gone. He gave five bags of silver to one, two bags of silver to another, and one bag of silver to the last—dividing it in proportion to their abilities. He then left on his trip.

"The servant who received the five bags of silver began to invest the money and earned five more. The servant with two bags of silver also went to work and earned two more. But the servant who received the one bag of silver dug a hole in the ground and hid the master's money.

"After a long time their master returned from his trip and called them to give an account of how they had used his money. The servant to whom he had entrusted the five bags of silver came forward with five more and said, 'Master, you gave me five bags of silver to invest, and I have earned five more.'

"The master was full of praise. 'Well done, my good and faithful servant. You have

been faithful in handling this small amount, so now I will give you many more responsibilities. Let's celebrate together!'

"The servant who had received the two bags of silver came forward and said, 'Master, you gave me two bags of silver to invest, and I have earned two more.

"The master said, 'Well done, my good and faithful servant. You have been faithful in handling this small amount, so now I will give you many more responsibilities. Let's celebrate together!'

"Then the servant with the one bag of silver came and said, 'Master, I knew you were a harsh man, harvesting crops you didn't plant and gathering crops you didn't cultivate. I was afraid I would lose your money, so I hid it in the earth. Look, here is your money back.'

"But the master replied, 'You wicked and lazy servant! If you knew I harvested crops I didn't plant and gathered crops I didn't cultivate, why didn't you deposit my money in the bank? At least I could have gotten some interest on it.'

"Then he ordered, 'Take the money from this servant, and give it to the one with the ten bags of silver. To those who use well what they are given, even more will be given, and they will have an abundance. But from those who do nothing, even what little they have

will be taken away."

In this passage there was a wealthy man (Jesus later referred to him as a "master"). He must have had a keen business sense because, as he was leaving to go on a long journey, he still desired to increase his wealth. He chose to call three other men to himself and distribute resources to them with the anticipation that they will grow what he gave them.

The first man received 5 bags of silver. This man went right to work. He probably woke up early to check the stock prices of the day. I'm sure that he spent time calling individuals, trying his best to convince them to invest with him. He was concentrated on the task given to him. He chose not to waste his time. He was intentional. As a result, he doubled his money from five bags of silver to ten.

The second man did not receive as much as the first. However, he took what he had received and moved forward with the same tenacity as the man with five bags of silver. Like the first man, this man was focused and intentional. He, too, doubled his money, going from two bags of silver to four bags.

But the third man thought about his opportunity differently. Instead of considering how he could take his silver and double it, he did nothing with his gift. He chose to bury the money into the ground. He didn't lose anything, but he didn't gain anything either. He stayed the same.

The master returned from his long journey wanting to hear an account for how the men handled his money. He went to the first man who received five bags of silver and asked him what he did with them. The man replied, "Master, you gave me five bags of silver to invest, and I have earned five more." The master exclaimed, "Well done, my good and faithful servant. You have been faithful in handling this small amount, so now I will give you many more responsibilities. Let's celebrate together!"

Next, he went to the man who received two bags of silver and asked him what he did with them. The man replied, "Master, you gave me two bags of silver to invest, and I have earned two more." The master exclaimed, "Well done, my good and faithful servant. You have been faithful in handling this small amount, so now I will give you many more responsibilities. Let's celebrate together!"

Finally, the master went to the man who had only received one bag of silver. He asked him what he did with it. The man replied, "Master, I knew you were a harsh man, harvesting crops you didn't plant and gathering crops you didn't cultivate. I was afraid I would lose your money, so I hid it in the earth. Look, here is your money back." The master went on and said, "You wicked and lazy servant! If you knew I harvested crops I didn't plant and gathered crops I didn't cultivate, why didn't you deposit my money in the bank? At least I could have gotten some interest on it." Then he ordered, "Take the money from this servant, and give it to the one with the ten bags of silver. To those who use well what they are given, even more will be given, and they will have an abundance. But from those who do nothing, even what little they have will be taken away."

The master was obviously upset at the way the man handled his money. He called him two things. One of the names was *"lazy."* This adjective I understand. The man was lazy! While the other two were waking up early, meeting with people, remaining focused and intentional, this man just buried his gift. He literally dug a hole in the ground and then went home to relax. Lazy!

However, the other adjective that the master used in describing his behavior was *"wicked."* What?! Wicked?! He might have been lazy, but to call him wicked is an astounding accusation. Why would the master call him wicked? Did he steal his master's money? No. Did he commit a crime? No. Did he do something immoral? No. What's so wrong about digging a hole in the ground and giving the money back?

The word *"wicked"* here, in the original Greek language, [2] is described as being "of a bad nature, or condition, in an ethical sense." Compared to the good and faithful, he who did nothing was labeled wicked and lazy. He was not wicked because he didn't produce as much as the one who had been given five. He was wicked because he didn't try to improve what he was given. The Pulpit commentary describes it this way:

> "In marked contrast with the commendation, *"good and faithful,"* he was *"wicked,"* in that he falsely accused his master, who really seems to have been ready to acknowledge the least service done to him, and never looked for results beyond a man's ability and opportunities. He was 'slothful,' not making an effort to improve the one talent entrusted to him."[3]

Therefore, one can gather from this word that God *demands* that we use what we have been given. Our life, and the gifts inside us all, are to be used for His glory and the advancement of His kingdom. He expects that you produce on the life

---

[2] Visit http://biblehub.com/greek/4190.htm for reference.
[3] Visit http://biblehub.com/commentaries/matthew/25-26.htm.

that you have been given.

Some of us think that our life is our own and we can live it the way we want, with no accountability. Often, with this attitude of living, we choose to live a sinful, selfish life, with no thought of offending a Holy God. We are sadly mistaken. First of all, we did not decide when we would arrive to earth. We just know that we were born whatever year we were born. We didn't decide who our parents were going to be. We didn't get to choose the family we would come into. We didn't even get to pick what eye color we would have. What makes us think that we can then decide how to live?

Oh, yes, God gives free will. He allows us to choose how we will live. But there is a way that He is expecting us to follow. And He will hold us accountable for our actions. Others go through their whole life, not doing anything wrong, yet not being productive. This, too, is a failure.

Chapter 2: The 5th Grader

Imagine a 5th grade class taking a test on a Friday. It's a typical 5th grade classroom. The children's desks are set up in straight rows across the room. There is a red, white and blue American flag up front near the blackboard. Their teacher is sitting at her desk with her head down reading a book while the students are taking a test. There's a student in the middle of the classroom named Billy. Billy hasn't even turned the test over to see the first question. Even though his teacher is at the front of the class, she is not aware of the distractions going on during the test.

Directly behind Billy are two students shooting spitballs at each other. To his right sits a student with his cell phone out, checking sports scores and the latest fashion on Google. And to the left of him there is a student who is reading some of the answers off of a cheat sheet he made the night before.

Billy said nothing and did nothing for his own test. He simply sat there while the test was being taken. At the end of the class, the teacher called for the tests to be turned in. Like all the other students, Billy went to the front of the classroom, placed his on her desk, and went home.

The following day the students came and sat down in their desks, uniformly, as usual. The teacher began to give back the graded tests. When Billy received his, he saw a large red letter F in the upper right corner. Billy couldn't believe it. He exclaimed, "Teacher, why did I get an F? I didn't do anything wrong. You didn't see it, but while your class was taking the test yesterday, the two kids behind me were shooting spitballs at each other, another kid was wasting time on his phone, and another one of your students was cheating. I sat here quietly, minding my own business. Why did I receive an F?" The teacher thought for a few seconds, and then replied, "Billy, you received an F not because you did something wrong, but because you didn't do anything."

God is serious about your life. He has given you your life to make a difference. The gifts and talents that you have received are for a specific purpose. 1 Peter 4:10 (NKJV) says, *"As each one has received a gift, minister it to one another, as good stewards of the manifold grace of God."* When we use our gifts we are good stewards of what has been given to us. You are one of a kind. There is no one on this earth like you. Others need you to use what you have. Others need to be uplifted by you. You have something to give, so give it!

During the test there were many distractions coming against the little 5th grader. Spitballs, internet activity, and cheat sheets were all reasons for Billy to sit there and do nothing. Are there any distractions keeping you from accomplishing great things in your life? Billy saw some kids cheating- are you distracted by others who are cheating you?

Time-Wasting Opportunities

In life we have many opportunities to be offended. Sometimes, when an offense comes, the people who have done us wrong are not even thinking about the incident, yet it could occupy our lives. Is there someone or something that is occupying your time, creativity, and energy? Is there anything in your heart that is not allowing you to move forward to being all God has intended you to be, and accomplishing all that God has for you? Is there someone 'cheating' you?

In Matthew chapter 18 the Bible clearly tells us how we should handle offense: *"If another believer sins against you, go privately and point out the offense. If the other person listens and confesses it, you have won that person back. But if you are unsuccessful, take one or two others with you and go back again, so that everything you say may be confirmed by two or three witnesses. If the person still refuses to listen, take your case to the church. Then if he or she won't accept the church's decision, treat that person as a pagan or a corrupt tax collector,"* (Matthew 18:15-17 NLT). Do you need to go to someone who has offended you?

The truth is, none of us are perfect. Not one of us! We have all done things that we shouldn't have. We have all done things that have hurt other people. We have all done things that have offended God. God, however, has forgiven us a tremendous debt. The debt of our own selfishness and sin. His grace is so merciful towards us. Do we really have the right to hold other people to offense and unforgiveness? When you consider the debt of your own sin, consider this parable of the "Unmerciful Servant" that Jesus told in Matthew 18:21-35:

Matthew 18:21-35 (NLT)

"Then Peter came to him and asked, "Lord, how often should I forgive someone who sins against me? Seven times?"

"No, not seven times," Jesus replied, "but seventy times seven!

"Therefore, the Kingdom of Heaven can be compared to a king who decided to bring his accounts up to date with servants who had

borrowed money from him. In the process, one of his debtors was brought in who owed him millions of dollars. He couldn't pay, so his master ordered that he be sold—along with his wife, his children, and everything he owned—to pay the debt.

But the man fell down before his master and begged him, 'Please, be patient with me, and I will pay it all.' Then his master was filled with pity for him, and he released him and forgave his debt.

But when the man left the king, he went to a fellow servant who owed him a few thousand dollars. He grabbed him by the throat and demanded instant payment.

"His fellow servant fell down before him and begged for a little more time. 'Be patient with me, and I will pay it,' he pleaded. But his creditor wouldn't wait. He had the man arrested and put in prison until the debt could be paid in full.

"When some of the other servants saw this, they were very upset. They went to the king and told him everything that had happened. Then the king called in the man he had forgiven and said, 'You evil servant! I forgave you that tremendous debt because you pleaded with me. Shouldn't you have mercy on your fellow servant, just as I had mercy on you?' Then the angry king sent the man to prison to be tortured until he had paid *his entire debt.*

"That's what my heavenly Father will do to you if you refuse to forgive your brothers and sisters from your heart."

Always remember that you have been forgiven much through Christ Jesus. Therefore, you are free to forgive others. The byproduct of such an attitude is that no one can cheat you out of a heart filled with joy and purpose!

Back to Billy's story… others in the class were choosing to waste time on the internet. The internet, smartphones, TV, computers, and any other electronic device are incredible tools for advancing your mission. However, they can also be incredible time wasters.

At the time of the writing of this book, smartphones and social media seem to be some of the greatest time wasters of this generation, especially among young people. Carolyn Gregorie of the Huffington Post reported that, "Young adults use their smart phones roughly twice as much as they estimate that they do. In fact, the (studies found) that these young adults use their phones on average of 5 hours a day. That's roughly one third of their total waking hours."[4]

---

[4] Carolyn Gregorie, "You Probably Use Your Smart Phone Way More Than You Think," Huffington Post.

I'm not sure how technology has progressed from the writing of this book to the time that you are reading this today, but one thing is for certain: time wasting opportunities are everywhere. When I was a young child there were many statistics and fears about how many hours kids were wasting in front of the T.V. In 2018, during the writing of this book, the statistics are currently geared towards smart phones, social media, the internet, etc. What are the time-wasting opportunities of your generation? What is attempting to rob you of the short life that you have left?

Remember, you only have a stack of hours left. And every day you have to hand over 24 of those hours, every week 168 hours, and every year 8,760. The truth is, distractions will come. Either by way of offense, or by many time-wasting opportunities. Again, the Bible shares that to be lazy is to be slothful, and to be slothful is to be wicked. To waste your life is a travesty. To do nothing is just as much a failure as doing wrong. The key is to remain focused on what really matters. But how do you discover what matters most?

Chapter 3: Driven by Success [Becoming]

Let's say that you have now discovered that time is precious, and you desire to do much with your life. But you are asking questions like, what really matters? Or, how do I discover the purpose of which I am here for? And what is success? There are perhaps as many definitions of success as there are people on the earth.

Everybody has a version of success! Some people may think that graduating at the top of their class is success. Others, think being the CEO of their company proves they are successful. Some are content with being a good, stay-at-home mom, satisfied in raising their children and taking care of their household.

In many foreign cultures, if someone feels they are not deemed as being successful, they take their own life. However, suicide in America has a strong grip on our lives as well. At the writing of this book, The American Foundation for Suicide Prevention reports that suicide is the 10th leading cause of death in the US. Each year, 44,193 people die by their own hand. That's 121 people a day, every day.

Men die by suicide 3.5 times more often than women, and white males account for 70% of the suicides. Among all the classes of people, the highest rate of suicides are during the middle age years.[5]

Psychology Today published an article titled "Six Reasons Why Individuals Choose Suicide."[6] They noticed that there are 6 reasons, or categories, of why people commit suicide. Without going into all six reasons, the thread that connects them all together was that most suicide victims simply didn't want to go on living. It wasn't that they wanted to die; the pain of living proved too great for them. I just want to tell somebody today that life is good. There is hope, and that you have a purpose and a destiny. You *can* discover what it is to be successful!

My definition of success is this: Becoming the person God created you to be, and doing what God created you to do. There are, essentially, two parts

---

[5] "Suicide Rate is up 1.2 Percent According to Most Recent CDC Data (2016)," American Foundation for Suicide Prevention. https://afsp.org/suicide-rate-1-8-percent-according-recent-cdc-data-year-2016/ (Accessed February 13, 2018).

[6] Dr. Wendy Boring-Bray, "Six Reasons Why People Choose Suicide," Psychology Today. www.psychologytoday.com/blog/new-beginning/201702/six-reasons-why-individuals-choose-suicide (February 13, 2018).

to this definition. 1.) *Becoming* the person God wants you to become, and 2.) *Doing* what God wants you to do; *becoming* and *doing*.

The First Step: Becoming

If the first step in being successful is "becoming," then how do you do that? And what does that even mean? The prophet Isaiah had an experience that truly transformed his life. The insights found here can also do the same for you. Consider Isaiah's vision of heaven:

Isaiah 6:1-9 (NLT)

"It was in the year King Uzziah died that I saw the Lord. He was sitting on a lofty throne, and the train of his robe filled the Temple. Attending him were mighty seraphim, each having six wings. With two wings they covered their faces, with two they covered their feet, and with two they flew. They were calling out to each other, "Holy, holy, holy is the LORD of Heaven's Armies! The whole earth is filled with his glory!" Their voices shook the Temple to its foundations, and the entire building was filled with smoke. Then I said, "It's all over! I am doomed, for I am a sinful man. I have filthy lips, and I live among a people with filthy lips. Yet I have seen the King, the LORD of Heaven's Armies." Then

one of the seraphim flew to me with a burning coal he had taken from the altar with a pair of tongs. He touched my lips with it and said, "See, this coal has touched your lips. Now your guilt is removed, and your sins are forgiven." Then I heard the Lord asking, "Whom should I send as a messenger to this people? Who will go for us?" I said, "Here I am. Send me." And he said, "Yes, go, and say to this people…"

This is a crazy passage of scripture; a scene that could be the highlight of any movie. There are angels shouting, buildings shaking, and smoke. The first thing that is important to notice is that Isaiah had an encounter with God. It says that, "In the year king Uzzah died I saw the Lord." In order for you to know your worth and value, you must see the Lord. He is looking at you right now. In fact, He is thinking about you constantly. Psalm 139:17-18 (NKJV) says, *"How precious also are Your thoughts to me, Oh God! How great is the sum of them! If I should count them, they would be more in number than the sand…"* Picture that in your mind right now: every grain of sand, on all the beaches and all the deserts on the whole earth. That's a lot of sand, and that's how many thoughts God is thinking about you!

It is so vital for you to understand that He is constantly thinking about you. Once you understand that God loves you in a magnificent way, you begin to grow your inner strength and confidence. Many people today believe that God does not love them. Thus, they don't have love for themselves. It's hard to begin being successful if you don't have this understanding.

The scriptures also say that when Isaiah saw God he saw Him "High and lifted up." This means Isaiah saw the Lord in His rightful place. He did not see God low and underserving of praise. But God was, and is, in THE place of authority. Our society today doesn't want to see God in the place of absolute authority. We would rather be the ones in control. We've kicked him out of our schools, our houses, our courts, and even our nations. We don't want him at the PTA, neighborhood associations, or potluck parties. Once a person, or people, step out from under the protection of God, they are all alone. They're like a city without walls, very vulnerable and unprotected. However, when one comes under God, they gain everything He has. His protection, His healing, His provision, etc. It's all found under Him!

Tonight, before you go to bed, look up at all the stars in the dark sky. Look at the moon and the planets. The Bible shares that God hung all the stars and placed the planets in their rightful place. The Bible also says, *"The heavens proclaim the glory of God. The skies display his craftsmanship.*

Day after day they continue to speak; night after night they make him known. They speak without a sound or word; their voice is never heard. Yet their message has gone through the earth, and their words to all the world." (Psalm 19:1-4 NLT) My wife loves these thoughts of scripture. They bring her confidence in who her God is, because if He has that much power, He is well able to handle the situations of life. Therefore, come under God. Believe that He has your best interest in mind, in every situation.

As a result of this encounter, Isaiah saw the holiness of God, and the ugliness of his own sin. Verse 6:5 says, *"Then I said, wow is me for I am undone and have filthy lips."* The prophet expresses the normal result of man's self-consciousness when in the presence of God. Moses hid his face and was afraid to even look upon God (Exodus 3:6). Job abhorred himself and repented in dust and ashes (Job 42:6). Peter fell down at the Lord's feet and cried, *"Depart from me, for I am a sinful man, O Lord."* (Luke 5:8 NIV) When you see God, for all He is worth, and all He is, you understand the frailty of your own humanity. This puts you in a state where you begin to lay yourself out on the dependence of God. The results of this type of encounter is where you can begin to receive the power of God to change your life.

Following this encounter, one of the angels

took a coal from the altar, brought it to Isaiah and touched his lips with it. This touch changed everything for him. Notice that Isaiah had been prophesying for the first five chapters of the book, this encounter was in the sixth chapter. But as a result of the touch from God he began to prophesy at a whole new dimension.

Whatever God touches is good. When Jesus changed the water into wine they called it *"the best"* (John, Chapter 2 NIV). When God created the Earth, He stood back and *"saw that it was good."* (Genesis, Chapter 1 NLT) They said of Jesus, *"Everything he does is wonderful."* (Mark 7:37 NLT) That's what God wants to do in your life. He wants to make it better and more effective. He wants you to parent at a whole new dimension, work on a more efficient level, become more effective in your studies, etc.

God has placed you on this earth for a purpose. You are not just here to take up space, live for 85 years, and then go back into the ground without any impact on humanity. I don't care what you do. I just want you to find what God has created you to do. And the first step in finding out what He has created you to do is to see Him "high and lifted up." You must see God. Because if you do, you will become undone in His presence, thus opening yourself up to a transformational touch from God.

In his book "If," Mark Batterson shares this story:

"Kay Kostopoulos teaches a class called 'Acting with Power' at the Stanford Graduate School of business.

At the beginning of each semester, her first assignment sets the stage for the class. She pairs off students randomly, then instructs them to stare at each other for three minutes without saying a word.

As you can imagine, the first few seconds are quite awkward. It's one thing staring into the eyes of someone you know, someone you love. It's quite another thing doing a three-minute stare-down with a complete stranger.

But Kostopoulos has found that something almost mystical happens during the exercise. After a few seconds, students lose self-consciousness as they focus their full attention on the face of the other person. They discover that this stranger's face tells a story. It exposes whether they've consistently used sunscreen or not. It's easy to tell if someone has had acne or a case of the chicken pox. Then there are the scars, which raise questions. And, of course, the smile lines frown lines, and worry lines that reveal a thin slice of history and personality."[7]

---

[7] Mark Batterson, *If: Trading Your Only Regrets for God's What If Possibilities* (Grand Rapids: Baker Books, 2015), 253.

Mark went on to share remarks similar to this:

What would happen if you did this exercise with Jesus Christ? What would it reveal? I believe that you would first notice the jagged tattoo across his forehead that was left from them placing the crown of thorns on him. If you were to see his smile lines by his eyes and lips, you would see the marks of someone who reclined at tables and laughed with sinners. As you make your way to his eyes, oh, how you would see the fire. A fire that was so passionate the day they turned his house to a den of thieves when He cried out, *"My house shall be called a house of Prayer,"* (Matthew 21:13 NKJV). But not only would you find fire in his eyes, you would also find tears of grace and mercy. Tears that wept for his friend Lazarus, and eyes that bestowed grace on Peter.

This Jesus that you are looking at now also died for you. In fact, if you were the only person on the earth He would have gone through all of that suffering, just for you. And He is also looking at you with grace and mercy. Because of this, He is so good, and worthy of your whole life. Let him have your life and allow him to shape you into the person He has called you to become. For becoming the person that God wants you to be is the first step in being successful.

Chapter 4: Doing - The Second Aspect of Being Successful

When I was in my early twenties I was a part of my church's worship team, playing my saxophone in the weekend services. At the same time I helped out in the youth ministry on Wednesday nights. Everything in my life was nice and orderly: the youth on Wednesdays and the worship team on Sundays. Until one day the youth pastor asked me to assist in the youth discipleship classes in the back portables of the property... On Sunday mornings. I obviously couldn't be on the stage playing my sax and in the portables teaching the Bible at the same time. This was a dilemma for me because I loved playing my instrument on the worship team, and I was beginning to love building into the lives of young people. However, I was content to do whatever God wanted me to do. The problem was that I couldn't discern where God would have me serve. I remember getting so frustrated with the fact that I could not discover what the right decision was that I even began to cry. I shouted at God, "Just tell me what to do and I'll do it Lord! Both opportunities are good, just direct me and I'll go!" Nothing. I later decided to quit the worship team, and start teaching the Bible. It ended up being one of the best decisions of my life. While I still play my saxophone from time to time, teaching the Bible is one of the most central pieces of my existence on this earth. That decision to teach a few teenagers the Bible has grown me to the ability to teach many people from all walks of life.

It's important to understand that God has a specific plan for your life. He has something on this earth that you are to fulfill. You are like an arrow that God wants to take out of his quiver and point to a specific target. You are not just a random accident. You are a gift and have a purpose, a vision from God himself. He told the prophet Jeremiah, *"Before I formed you in the womb I knew you; before you were born I sanctified you; I ordained you a prophet to the nations."* (Jeremiah 1:5 NKJV) The Prophet Isaiah said, *"The Lord called me before my birth; from within the womb he called me by name. He made my words of judgment as sharp as a sword. He has hidden me in the shadow of his hand. I am like a sharp arrow in his quiver... And now the Lord speaks- the one who formed me in my mother's womb to be his servant, who commissioned me to bring Israel back to him."* (Isaiah 49:1-2, 5 NLT)

The question of life is not what can I do? It's what should I do? I can do a lot of things. I can start a business, be a missionary, go to school and become a doctor, be a stay at home parent. I can do a lot of things. But what's most important is not what *I* want to do, it's what does *God* want me to do. Jesus said, *"Not everyone who says to Me, 'Lord, Lord,' Shall enter the kingdom of heaven, but he who does the will of My Father in heaven."* (Matthew 7:21 NKJV) So what is the will of God? The will of God is simply *God's choice*. What does God choose for this relationship, job opportunity, career path, possible person to marry, etc.

Sometimes it can be very difficult to discern these things. You might have found yourself like I was, shouting at God, "Just tell me what to do and I'll do it Lord!" I believe there are ways that you can grow in discerning God's choice in your life. First it begins with your heart attitude. Do you desire God's will over your own? Do you want God's choice over yours?

Lucifer (who later became Satan) had a great position in heaven. He was the chief worship leader. His job was to lead all of heaven in worship to God. It was a pretty nice job. No one was like him. He had honor, prestige and the greatest privilege: leading worship in heaven. However he was not satisfied. He did not submit to the will of

God and it turned out pretty bad for him. As soon as he thought, *"I will ascend to heaven and set my throne above God's stars. I will preside on the mountain of the gods"* (Isaiah 14:13 NLT). Jesus said, *"I saw Satan fall like lightening from heaven"* (Luke 10:18 NIV). And He was cast down to the earth.

You have to lay your life down before God. I'm not talking about what socks to wear or praying if you should brush your teeth. Some things we just know we should do. But what about which job to take? Which school should I go to? Who should I marry? How many children should I have? Which house should I buy? These decisions are ones that you need the Holy Spirit directing and guiding you through. Having the heart attitude of submitting these decisions to the Holy Spirit is the first step to growing in your discernment of God's choice.

The second area which you can grow in is filling yourself up with the Word of God. There once was an ancient city. This city had a tremendous amount of commerce flowing through it. High buildings, newspapers, new businesses, created a vibrancy and excitement that filled the air. You could almost smell the dreams of the people coming true. Anything that the people wanted or needed seemed available to them. However, in the outskirts of the metropolis there was a small country town where the people did not lavish in the luxuries of their sister city. Yet in the center of this town was a beautiful grey cobblestone well where people who lived in the country would come to draw water. As they dipped their pots and gathered the water, it would give life to their whole household. It was everything they needed. When they were hungry it allowed them to cook food. When they were dirty it allowed them to clean their cloths. When they were thirsty it allowed them to be refreshed. All of this came from the well. But in order for the well to be useful it needed to have water. Without the water the well was useless. Your spirit is also a well, and the Word of God and prayer are the water that fills that well. As you fill your spirit with the Word of God and prayer you will be able to draw on that which you have put in. This is a major key for your success.

The Bible says that the Word of God brings life to your life. Proverbs 4:20-22 (NLT) says, *"My child, pay attention to what I say. Listen carefully to my words. Don't lose sight of them. Let them penetrate deep into your heart, for they bring life to those who find them, and healing to their whole body."* I have heard that there are over 5,000 promises in the Bible. As you begin to read the Bible more and more, your heart begins to be filled up. Like a blue balloon that expands with every breath you breathe into it, so your heart is expanded with the promises of God every time you store them. Over time, as you fill your heart up, you actually move from having promises to being a promise. You become so filled with promise that you become a walking breathing promise on the earth. Ask yourself this question: How would your life be different if you had more of the promises of God in your heart?

The Word of God also balances our own voice. Sometimes it is hard to discover the voice of the Lord. The Bible says that, *"God is not a man, so he does not lie. He is not human, so he does not change his mind. Has he ever spoken and failed to act? Has he ever promised and not carried it through?"* (Numbers 23:19 NLT) Therefore, He will never contradict his Word. That's why you need the scriptures to guide you! If you feel He is telling you to do something, but it goes against scripture, you can know you are not hearing correctly. I had a friend once tell me he was so upset with his wife that he wanted to kill her. He was of course saying it in jest, and we had a good laugh. But we both knew it wasn't right for him to kill his spouse because God says in the Ten Commandments, *"You shall not murder."* (Exodus 20:13 NKJV) So if God said, *"You shall not murder,"* you know He cannot be telling you to kill someone because that would go against His word. This is a rather silly example because most people understand, even inherently, that murder is wrong. But what about other areas that are not so clear to our society. For example, sleeping with a boyfriend or girlfriend, smoking marijuana, or homosexuality. Are you "allowed" to do these things? What if you "feel" in your heart they are right? How can you grow in discerning the voice of God for your own life?

If you want to maximize your time on earth, prayer is something you must engage with. Martin Luther once said, "If I fail to spend two hours in prayer each morning, the devil gets the victory through the day. I have so much business I cannot get on without spending three hours daily in prayer."[8] In fact, spending time in prayer is one of the absolute best ways to spend your time. Prayer does several things for you. It shapes your character, refreshes your spirit, and gives you direction.

Prayer Shapes Your Character.

Prayer shapes your character in a positive way. As you sit in the presence of God you become transformed into His glory. If you were to sit in a smoke-filled bar, after a while, your clothes would smell like smoke. In the same way, the incense of heaven is a glorious smell working on your soul as

---

[8] E.M. Bounds, *The Preacher and Prayer* (Asheville: Revival Literature), 40.

you spend time with God in prayer. After a while God's "smell" will get onto you. E.M. Bounds said, "It is prayer-force which makes saints. Holy characters are formed by the power of real praying. The more of true saints, the more of praying; the more of praying, the more of true saints."[9] David prayed in Psalm 51:10 (NLT), *"Create in me a clean heart, O God. Renew a loyal spirit within me."* The hopeful part about this verse is that he wrote it during a time of deep repentance. David had messed up big time. In fact, this poem was written during the aftermath of the biggest mistake of his life. And yet, you can see the hope that even in your failures God can shape your character. I do not know what character flaws you have in your life. I don't know what areas have been a stronghold against you. But I do know that by the Spirit of God, through prayer, you can be shaped into who He wants you to be. Don't lose hope, just commit to prayer.

Prayer Refreshes Your Spirit.

One of the worst things in life is to be downcast and drained. The sun could be shining today and the birds chirping outside your window, but if there is darkness in your soul it doesn't make it a sunny day for you. However, if you have a

---

[9] E.M. Bounds, *Power Through Prayer* (Grand Rapids: Zondervan Publishing House, 1962), 48.

light in your heart you can go a long way on the journey. Prayer brings a refreshing from within. Philippians 4:6-7 (NLT) says, *"Don't worry about anything; instead, pray about everything. Tell God what you need, and thank him for all he has done. Then you will experience God's peace, which exceeds anything we can understand. His peace will guard your hearts and minds as you live in Christ Jesus."* Also, Psalm 23:1-3 (NIV) reads, *"The Lord is my shepherd, I lack nothing. He makes me lie down in green pastures, he leads me beside quiet waters, he refreshes my soul. He guides me along the right paths for his name's sake."* So many people in the world today are looking for peace. Most people are looking to the wrong things to bring this inner happiness. Remember, God is the one who made you. He formed your, *"inward (most) parts."* (Psalm 139:13 NKJV) Therefore, He knows you inside and out. He knows what will bring you the most peace. Spend time with Him, be refreshed by Him, so that you can run this race of life with purpose and destiny.

Prayer Gives You Direction.

In life you will have many decisions to make. There will be many choices. Most of them will sound good, but the key is to discern which one is the best choice: God's choice. Jesus was a man of prayer. He sought the Father's guidance early and often. In Luke 6:12-16, Jesus had a big decision to make. At this time of His earthly ministry, He had many disciples and followers. Yet it was His desire to gather a smaller number of men that He could disciple. The men that He would gather to himself would later become the apostles of the early church. How did He know which men to draw out from the massive crowd, the men that would become His greatest companions? In this passage, the Bible shows that before picking these men, He went up to the mountain and prayed all night to get the answer. My goodness! Have you ever prayed all night for one answer? Staying up all night in prayer for an answer is a big commitment. However, one can clearly see how Jesus operated, pressed into prayer, and received His answer. I am glad that Christ took His time in prayer with this decision because it literally change the world.

Life is like a game of chess. Many moves are complicated and it's hard to see the end from the beginning. However, God knows all things, and He knows the moves that are best for you. Learning how to trust God, and developing the art of hearing His voice inside of you, will help you make the best move almost every time. So, press into prayer and allow the voice of God to speak to your heart, to guide and direct you, and lead you in the right way.

The secret to great praying is long praying.

Like a long warm bath soothes the body and soul, so long times spent in the presence of God enhances the spirit. E.M. Bound said, "Much time spent with God is the secret of all successful praying. Prayer which is felt as a mighty force is the mediate or immediate product of much time spent with God." William Wilberforce accomplished much with his time on earth. E.M. Bounds quotes Wilberforce:

"This perpetual hurry of business and company ruins me in soul if not in body. More solitude and earlier hours! I suspect I have been allotting habitually too little time to religious exercises, as private devotion and religious meditation, Scripture-reading, etc. Hence I am lean and cold and hard. I had better allot two hours or an hour and a half daily. I have been keeping too late hours, and hence have had but a hurried half hour in a morning to myself. Surely the experience of all good men confirms the proposition that without a due measure of private devotions the soul will grow lean. But all may be done through prayer- almighty prayer, I am ready to say- and why not? For that it is almighty is only though the gracious ordination of the God of love and truth. O then, pray, pray, pray!"[10]

---

[10] E.M. Bounds, *The Preacher and Prayer* (Asheville: Revival Literature), 83.

God is looking for a generation of people who voraciously rise up and seek His face in prayer. "What the Church needs today is not more machinery or better, not new organizations or more and novel methods, but men whom the Holy Ghost can use- men of prayer men mighty in prayer. The Holy Ghost does not flow through methods, but through men. He does not come on machinery, but on men. He does not anoint plans, but men- men of prayer."[11]

Young person I'm writing to you now to tell you that if you want to leave a lasting impact on this earth now and for eternity, you must become a person of prayer! Get into a church that teaches on prayer. Get a mentor who prays. Get connected to a church that has a prayer meeting. Our sending church, Trinity Church International, had two daily prayer meetings 5 days a week! It was there, and through the leadership and culture of the church, that I caught the spirit of prayer in my own life. Prayer has made the difference for me, and it will for you too, as it has for centuries.

---

[11] E.M. Bounds, *Power Through Prayer* (Grand Rapids: Zondervan Publishing House, 1962), 12.

Chapter 5: Where Our Culture is Missing It

Sleeping Around

Ephesians 5:3 (NIV)

"But among you there must not be even a hint of sexual immorality or of any kind of impurity, or of greed, because these are improper for God's holy people."

This is one of my favorite verses. I love the NIV version, especially, because it says, "there must not be *even a hint* of sexual immorality." This is such a powerful statement because it really cuts through to our thoughts, intentions, and actions. While the culture may be saying, "Do what you want, do what feels good, and get as close to the line as you can." God is saying, "Don't let there be even a hint of sin in your life!" What a radical statement! But it makes sense doesn't it? I mean, do you really think that Christ was whipped and flogged, His blood rising to the blue skies off his back, so much blood dripping from his skull that it filled His mouth, His naked body dropping off a wooden cross, just so you can push the limits of sexual immorality? No, of course not! He died so that you may become holy in His sight. So, walk like it. Talk like it. Be an example of it. Be sexually pure!

The thing about intimacy with the opposite sex before you are married is that God is trying to protect you. Sex is the most intimate thing you can do with another person. Whenever you leave your house you always put clothes on. Why do you put clothes on when you leave the house? Have you ever thought about going to school or to your job naked? Of course not! That's because being naked is a very intimate thing. Therefore, you do not "show" yourself to just anybody. The act of sex, where a man enters a woman through the sexual organs, is an *extremely* intimate moment. In fact, it is arguably the most intimate act two people can participate in. That is why God designed sex to be experienced with only one person. Sex is extremely private. Therefore it should not be shared with just anyone, but saved for your life-long marriage partner. If you are reading this book and you have already given yourself away before you have found your marriage partner, let me encourage you: you are not alone. Many people have failed in this area. The important thing for you to do now is to repent! Repent means to turn away and go in the opposite direction. If you have been walking in sexual promiscuity, I encourage you to start walking in the way of purity. Tell someone of your decision and ask them to hold you accountable.

Pornography

Remember the scripture that Paul wrote in Ephesians, *"Don't let there be even a hint of sexual immorality."* Well Jesus said, *"Anyone who even looks at a woman with lust has already committed adultery with her in his heart."* (Matthew 5:28 NLT) Therefore, we can sin, not only with our actions, but also with our eyes. This is why pornography is a sin.

When you watch pornography you are seeing two or more people act out a scene in a movie. The type of movie that you are watching is called a pornographic movie. Like in all movies, the scenes depicted in pornography are enhanced. Take Action films for example. A similar scene in these types of movies is often shown at the end where the good guy is trying to reach his prize (his wife, the treasure, or whatever). He is often tasked with entering an abandoned building and in between he and his prize are 50 bad guys with machine guns and machetes. Miraculously, the good guy moves through the building, killing all the bad guys with just a pistol. You get the picture. It is incredible that while we know this scenario could never happen in real life, we still love watching it. But even though we love to watch these types of scenes it is understood that they are not real, and in real life they could never be actualized. Action films, dramas, horror films, etc. The principle is still the same. They are enhanced pictures of real life.

Pornography is the same way. Porn is a movie or depiction of sexual acts. But it's a movie, or more importantly, it's an enhancement. Let me say it real clear: PORNOGRAPHY IS NOT REAL. Real people don't sound like that, bend like that, or act like that. The problem is, when people watch porn, they get a fantasy in their heads about how sex should be. Then when they discover sex with their spouse is not the same, they get upset, frustrated, and angry. The devil loves when people watch porn. Because he knows that eventually it will bring separation and a lack of intimacy within the marriage relationship.

When I was younger, my two brothers, 9 and 10 years old at the time, used to love to watch the Discovery Channel late at night. On this channel they would show African wildlife scenes. A lot of times they would watch action shots of lions attacking zebras or gazelles. It was interesting to watch as the lion would wait patiently as these herds would come near, and at the right moment, he would burst forth and scatter them. My brothers would marvel as they saw the lion chase these scared animals. The chase would go on until the herd, once closely connected, began to separate until there would be one lonely animal running a part from the crowd. Every time that happened, the lion devoured his prey. The Devil is trying to do the same with you. *"Be alert and of sober mind. Your enemy the devil prowls around like a roaring lion looking for someone to devour."* (1 Peter 5:8 NIV) The Devil wants to separate you: from godly friends, your spouse, and God. And he is using pornography as one of his greatest tools.

Porn also creates desires to look outside the marriage covenant. It dreams about what people are like in bed. It begins to take over your life. Listen to the wisdom from Proverbs:

Proverbs 5:15-19 (NLT)

"Drink water from your own well- share your love only with your wife. Why spill the water of your springs in the streets, having sex with just anyone? You should reserve it for yourselves. Never share it with strangers. Let your wife be a fountain of blessing for you. Rejoice in the wife of your youth. She is a loving deer, a graceful doe. Let her breasts satisfy you always. May you always be captivated by her love."

It goes on to say:

Proverbs 6:20-35 (NLT)

"My son, obey your father's commands, and don't neglect your mother's instruction. Keep their words always in your heart. Tie them around your neck. When you walk, their counsel will lead you. When you sleep, they will protect you. When you wake up, they will advise you. For their command is a lamp and their instruction a light; their corrective discipline is the way to life. It will keep you from the immoral woman, from the smooth tongue of a promiscuous woman. Don't lust for her beauty. Don't let her coy glances seduce you. For a prostitute will bring you to poverty, but sleeping with another man's wife will cost you your life. Can a man scoop a flame into his lap and not have his clothes catch on fire? Can he walk on hot coals and not blister his feet? So it is with the man who sleeps with another man's wife. He who embraces her will not go unpunished. Excuses might be found for a thief who steals because he is starving. But if he is caught, he must pay back seven times what he stole, even if he has to sell everything in his house. But the man who commits adultery is an utter fool, for he destroys himself. He will be wounded and disgraced. His shame will never be erased. For the woman's jealous husband will be furious, and he will show no mercy when he

takes revenge. He will accept no compensation, nor be satisfied with a payoff of any size."

What does all this have to do with time? EVERYTHING. If you are wasting hours that you have during the day to satisfy yourself in an ungodly manner, it is not making the best use of your time. Satan would love to have you entrapped in pornography while the people outside your door are going to hell. I encourage you to give yourself to God, to the purposes that He has for you. People need you. They need your pure imagination. Therefore, don't let there be even a hint of sexual immorality in your mind, spirit, and actions! If you feel you are caught in the trap of pornography please tell a trusted mentor or friend. The Bible says in James 5:16 (NIV), *"Therefore confess your sins to each other and pray for each other so that you may be healed,"* and in Romans 8:1 (NLT), *"There is no condemnation for those who are in Christ Jesus."* So if you need to, bring it into the light and be free!

Smoking Marijuana

At the writing of this book there is a huge political fight for the recreational use of marijuana. Colorado and several other states have already legalized it. There is a good chance that by the time you are reading this book all 50 states will have made smoking weed legal. Should you smoke it? Is it a sin for you to smoke weed? Does the Bible say anything about it? Again listen to the wisdom from Proverbs, and then follow my logic:

Proverbs 23:29-35 (NLT)

"Who has anguish? Who has sorrow? Who is always fighting? Who is always complaining? Who has unnecessary bruises? Who has bloodshot eyes? It is the one who spends long hours in the taverns, trying out new drinks. Don't gaze at the wine, seeing how red it is, how it sparkles in the cup, how smoothly it goes down. For in the end it bites like a poisonous snake; it stings like a viper. You will see hallucinations, and you will say crazy things. You will stagger like a sailor tossed at sea, clinging to a swaying mast. And you will say, "They hit me, but I didn't feel it. I didn't even know it when they beat me up. When will I wake up so I can look for another drink?"

Those are some strong words of wisdom concerning a substance that alters your mind. The interesting, and pivotal point of this passage is that alcohol was legal in this society. However, even though no one would go to jail for consuming this substance, the book of Proverbs is obviously highlighting the negative effects of it.

Perhaps the worst part of smoking weed, concerning your time, is that it often causes one to become too relaxed toward the purposes of God. As you puff the drug into your lungs, you are not only exhaling smoke out, but you are also blowing your dreams away. As that cloud of smoke dissipates into thin air, so your life is just passing away, one high after another. Don't waste your life on drugs! Your life is too short to pass away Friday after Friday. There is too much for you to do; your life matters too much to get caught up in the entanglement of being under the influence.

Often times, people who are on drugs do not concern themselves with the purposes of God. If you are engaging with these activities you are also entangling your heart to those around you who don't have the heart of God. It is God's will that you be holy and sober. It's not just about the drug itself, it's also about who you are spending your time with. You are called to run with giants! You are called to be a world changer, to make a difference. Put the drug down and pick up the mighty purpose of God!

The Apostle Paul said, *"You say, 'I am allowed to do anything'- but not everything is good for you. You say, 'I am allowed to do anything'- but not everything is beneficial."* (1 Corinthians 10:23 NLT) It would not be profitable for me to watch 10 hours of TV every day. I am allowed to do it. It isn't against the law for me to engage with T.V. this way. But if I watched T.V. for 10 hours a day, every day, it would be extremely harmful to my body, relationships, and life in general. You are a smart individual. Don't allow your friends or culture to dictate to you what you should do. Get the wisdom of God, and the direction of the Holy Spirit in your life, and let Him guide you into all things profitable.

These are just a few areas where the Bible can guide your life through the dark waves of the culture. But, again, it is important for you to find a daily rhythm of the reading of God's word, and of prayer, so that you might fill your spirit up with His promises and direction. When you are filled up with His voice you have His direction inside of you, and He will lead you to the right places for your life. So, reading the Word and prayer are essential first steps to being successful. But there is now more for you to build on…

Chapter 6: Where To Concentrate

As you saw with Billy the 5th grader, living a holy life is not enough to achieving what God has for you. Yes, living holy and being a person of prayer and the Word are pivotal first and complete steps that you need to take to be successful. However, there also needs to be a focus towards your destiny. As you now begin to step out into what the Lord would have for you, there are three areas that will need your attention: faithfulness, fruitfulness, and forgetfulness.

Faithfulness

Sometimes when people jump out to start something new it can be a while until they begin to see worthwhile results. It's in these times that many people become discouraged and give up. I like to say that we live in a microwave society, but we serve a crockpot God. God's promises, for the most part, take time to see results. The way God deals with a man is to take his time with him. Moses had to wait 40 years on the backside of a desert, herding sheep for his father-in-law, before

God called him from the burning bush. David had to hide in caves, running from King Saul who was trying to kill him for 13 years. Jesus was hidden for 30 years before his ministry went public. God is always working in these times of obscurity. The key is to be faithful and love him in all seasons of your life.

Other times the directions from God don't seem to make sense. In John, Chapter 2, Jesus performed his first miracle: turning the water into wine. You might remember the story. Jesus was at a wedding with his friends and family, and the hosts ran out of wine. The message got to Mary, Jesus' mother, and she told Jesus to create some more. Jesus was reluctant at first, but eventually He gave into his mother's request. Even the Son of God listens to his mother! When Jesus agreed to do it, Mary went to the servants working the wedding and said, "Do whatever He tells you." Jesus gave them a pretty weird request. He said, "Put water in the wine barrels." If you are just skimming the story, you might miss the preposterousness of this command. They were probably thinking to themselves, "This guy is crazy! We are out of wine, we don't need more water; we need more wine!" After they filled the pots with water they brought them to the master of ceremonies so that he could test the drink. As the master dipped his spoon into the pot, I'm sure the workers were thinking, "My goodness, we are going to get fired over this." As soon as the master tasted the fluid, he exclaimed, "This is better wine than the first batch!" The workers were relieved.

This is a story of just being faithful to what God has called you to. Don't worry what other people are thinking or doing, just be faithful to what you know to do. What is God calling you to do right now? Serve in a ministry at your church? Intern in the medical field? Start a business? Reach out to a neighbor? Write a book? Whatever it is, I'm sure that as you are faithful to follow the direction that God is speaking to you, you will see the miracles of God!

Fruitfulness

The second area that needs your attention is that of fruitfulness. 1 Peter 4:10 (NLT) says, *"God has given each of you a gift from his great variety of spiritual gifts. Use them well to serve one another."* My dad is an incredible builder. He just always had a gift for building things. He has built beautiful luxury homes for wealthy people, been involved in building a hospital in South Florida, and many other projects. Perhaps his most valued project was that of his lake cabin. The amazing thing about this cabin is that he built it by himself. Literally. Board by board, rock by rock, his hands put it together. Of course, my two brothers and I tried to help him from time to time. However, I don't think I was much help.

Sometimes I would go to the cabin on the weekends to help my dad. I remember one time I started putting up some of the dry wall and after about thirty seconds of him seeing me do my work he said, "Dan, please just get a broom and start sweeping in the corner." He must have saw in me the complete lack of ability to build things! And he would have saw correctly. I just don't have the ability to do that kind of work.

One of the keys to life is to discover your gifting and grow in it. I could, if I wanted to, get a job in construction. But because I am not gifted in that area I would come home day after day, discouraged and unfulfilled. However, I have other abilities. They lean more towards leadership, communication, pastoring, preaching, etc. The important thing for me is not to compare myself with my Dad, but to discover and develop *my* gifting. Many people struggle with the comparison trap. People struggle with comparison because they do not understand the importance of the gifts they've been given.

You have a gift from God. Psalm 139:14 (NKJV) says, *"I praise you because I am fearfully and wonderfully made."* God has fashioned you and created you as an awesome wonder - a God-given seed in the earth. Discover your gifts and then share them with the community around you for the glory of God.

Forgetfulness

The third area that needs your attention is to be forgetful. Isaiah 43:18-19 (NKJV) says, *"Do not remember the former things, nor consider the things of old. Behold, I will do a new thing, now it shall spring forth; shall you not know it? I will even make a road in the wilderness and rivers in the desert."* Sometimes things happen to people, by their own hand or someone else's, that can affect them negatively. These things can often stick to their soul like smoke on a jacket.

I used to know a saint of a woman. This woman was a person of complete joy, purity, and integrity. I knew her in the later years of her life. One day she told me that she did something that caused her 20 years of guilt. She carried guilt with her for 20 years! I was so surprised to hear that she struggled with this sort of pain in her early life because she seemed to live so free. She went on to tell me that she had received this freedom through the Word and Spirit of God working in her life. There will be times when mistakes happen in your life. Satan wants you to sit under the dark cloud of your pain. Yet God has opened the skies for the sun to shine on you. It's important that you move forward in God. He loves you, forgives you and still has a plan for you. He wants you to walk in freedom, so walk in it!

In 1991, Billy Crystal starred in a movie called, "City Slickers." In the movie, Billy's character was a middle-aged man who had not found deep fulfillment in his life. He was busy, had a wife, friends, some money, yet still lacked something. He came up with the idea to go on a trip to a ranch to 'get away, and find himself.' He thought that if he could just get out of the city where he lived, and went to a place of solace, it might help him discover himself. The ranch was what you might expect. Miles of open, western land. Cattle grazing on the hills, fire pits and horses. One day he was on horseback on an old, dirt road with the Rancher who ran the place. While they traveled the dusty road, the old man began to share how much he loved ranching life; it was his life. As they talked, Billy still seemed confused as to why he was not finding fulfillment for himself. The old rancher began to engage Billy with a conversation that went something like this:

"You know what your problem is?"
"No," Billy replied
"You guys are all the same. You spend 50 weeks a year getting your knot all tied up, and you think you can come out here and everything will be fixed," said the Rancher.
"Do you know what the secret to life is, son?"

Billy answered, "No, what's the secret?"

"One thing," the Rancher said, holding his finger up toward the sky.

"Well that's great, but what's the one thing?"

The rancher leaned in, "That's for you to discover."

Chapter 7: The Archer

In the 2016 Summer Olympic Games there were 11,237 athletes who participated in 306 events in 28 different sports. One of the most popular events in any Olympics is the 100-meter track meet. Runners from all over the world come and line up together, wait for the gun to go off, and then—with an incredible burst of energy and speed—take off towards the finish line.

Another of the most popular is swimming. Swimmers kick their legs viciously through the water, pushing themselves towards the final touch of the wall, many times a tenth of a second deciding gold or silver.

Gymnastics is a very popular sport as well. Gymnasts jump and twirl effortlessly in the air, defying gravity with even the slightest mistake possibly causing bodily harm.

We watch these sports with great anticipation and nervousness. Ecstasy is usually the outcome by the end of the event. These are stadium shaking, body vibrating events.

And then there is a sport that is quite different from all the others. It usually isn't on during the prime time T.V. hours. It's not held in a stadium and many people do not watch it. It's usually held in an open field in the back woods of the country. There are only a few elements to this sport: a man or woman, a bow and arrow in hand, focusing on one red target—Archery.

Unlike many of her athletic counterparts, the archer doesn't desire the flashing lights of a filled stadium, nor the cheering of fans and family. She needs focus for her target. Her goal is simple: hit the target. If she misses, even by a fraction, she must wait another four years to try for the prize again.

Your life is like this sport. You stand alone like the archer. Often there aren't stadiums of people shouting your name. In fact, most people in the world don't even know who you are. You have a target that you must hit if you are to be successful. But how do you hit it, and even more ambiguous, how do you discover the target? What should you be aiming at? Do you know? The secret to the archer is found in Psalm 37:4 (NKJV), which says, *"Delight yourself also in the Lord, and He shall give you the desires of your heart."*

For a long time I had a hard time understanding this verse. I didn't know what it meant when it said, *"Delight,"* or how He would give me the desires of my heart. What if I had the desire to get a Black Corvette, did God *have* to give it to me? How could I actualize these things, and were they pure desires?

The word *"delight"* here simply means to become intimate with God. The Message translation of the Bible says the phrase, *"Keep company with God."* The key here, to getting your desires actualized, is getting close to God, spending time with him, and growing your relationship with Him: delighting in Him. As you become intimate with God in a special way He, as in any intimate relationship, begins to drop his desires into your heart and his desires become your desires. Therefore, the Word can say that as you delight spending time with Him, He will give you the desires of your heart. But that's only because they were first His desires. They have only become yours as well through the process of delighting. And because they are His, He desires to also give them to you. Consider Matthew Henry's commentary on this verse:

"To delight in God is as much a privilege as a duty. He has not promised to gratify the appetites of the body, and the humors of the fancy, but the desires of the renewed, sanctified soul. What is the desire of the heart of a good man? It is this, to know, and love, and serve God. Commit thy way unto the Lord; roll thy way upon the Lord, so the margin reads it. Cast thy burden upon the Lord, the burden of thy care. We must roll it off ourselves, not afflict and perplex ourselves with thoughts about future events, but refer them to God. By prayer spread thy case and all thy cares before the Lord, and trust in him. We must do our duty, and then leave the event with God. The promise is very sweet: He shall bring that to pass, whatever it is, which thou has committed to him."[12]

As our life passes on and the stack of time grows smaller and smaller, we have to be sure that we are hitting our mark. Francis Chan once said, "Our greatest fear should not be of failure but of succeeding at things in life that don't really matter."[13]

I once heard John Bevere talk about the importance of doing what the Lord wants, not just what we think would be good to do with our lives. He gave the illustration of a lady who died and went to heaven. When she got there, she was a little surprised at St. Peter's demeanor in greeting her at the pearly gates. Peter had his head down,

---

[12] Visit http://biblehub.com/commentaries/psalms/37-4.htm.

[13] Michael Lukaszewski, *Streamline: How to Create Healthy Church Systems* (United States: Caufield & Finch Publishing).

looking like he was reading a book and didn't acknowledge her standing there. Finally, she said, "Is there something wrong, sir? On earth, I was an international best seller, traveling around the nation doing book tours, and helping to explain how people can have a better life on earth and make a difference for God's kingdom. What seems to be the problem?" St. Peter looked up from the book he was reading and replied, "That's true. While you were on earth you spent your days traveling, for weeks at a time, speaking and selling books. The problem is that God didn't call you to be an author, he called you to be a stay-at-home mom and raise your three boys, and those boys would have really changed the world."

In life you will have many choices. The key is not just picking whatever you think is best. The key is discerning what God thinks is best. You must understand that God sets the target for your life. Instead of wishing you had a different target, or comparing how your target matches up to the person next to you, you should spend more time practicing how you can hit the target God has set for you.

Chapter 8: The Farmer

The stages of life can be compared to a farmer who grew corn. There are three stages that the farmer has to go through. First, he has to dig his fields. Working with the strength of his back, he plows the hard, black dirt. From early in the morning, until the sun goes down, he works the ground to make sure the seed is planted correctly. As he watches and prays for rain, the crop eventually produces a harvest, but He is not finished.

The second stage is picking the harvest and cooking it for his family. This is also sacrificial. There are many days that he just wants to relax, but he knows his family needs food, so he continues to work hard in making sure the food is prepared properly. As the crop season ends he knows that he still has more work to do, and that is to teach the next generation to plant and cultivate the harvest. For if no one is teaching the next generation, how will the harvest continue to come in? And that is the third stage: reaching the next generation.

Some of you reading this book are in the first stage of life. You are in the foundational stages. I encourage you to work with all of your might. Give your youth to the Lord and He will take you far. So many youth are just "siting on the porch" thinking they have all the time in the world to do something. I heard TD Jakes say something to the effect of, "Youth goes like a runaway slave, it's here today and gone tomorrow, it's gone, gone, gone!" You better get up, and get to it!

Some of you are in the second stage of life. This can be a very sacrificial time period. A time where you are constantly giving and feeding others. It's in these seasons when we question a lot of decisions that we have made in our past, wondering how or if we could have made better decisions to affect our present situation. This is a time where we almost lose ourselves because we are giving out so much to our family. Let me encourage you today, if you are in this season of giving, don't stop and don't quit because those around you need you. You were made for this. You can do it!

Others are in the third stage. As you have read this book, understanding that your time left is very limited. I want to encourage you not to become dismayed. You have ran your own race and perhaps the best way for you to use your time is to reach out to those who are coming after you. Share how you did it and let them learn from you. For this could actually be your best and most impactful season. You still matter to this generation. We still need you. Every time we look at you we don't just see an "old person," we see someone who has gone before us, built something for us to stand on, and a testimony of God's goodness and grace. Yes, you still have something to give.

When I think about all the things discussed in this book. I think about the reason for our urgency. Yes, time is short. Yes, it is a sin to waste your life. And yes, you have a specific calling on your life. But there is a more important reason to do something with the time you have been given. John 3:16 (NKJV) says, *"For God so loved the world that he gave is only begotten son, that whoever believes in him should not perish but have everlasting life."* God is pretty concerned with the world. He gave His Son to be crucified on a cross. His back was beaten with whips: 39 times they lashed the skin off his back. His blood splatted across the blue skies. They took His head and smashed the crown of thorns across his forehead. Then they placed His naked body on a cross and pounded nails into His wrists and feet. As they lifted Him high into the air, He hung as a sacrifice for your sin and mistakes. Come to Him afresh and anew today. Call out to Him saying, "Dear Lord Jesus, thank you for giving your life for mine. Please forgive me for my sins and mistakes. I want to completely live for you. Today I choose Jesus, now and forever!"

If you have prayed this prayer for the first time, or in a repentant way, reach out to a Pastor, leader, mentor, or a Christian. Let them know that you are serious in following the Lord and want to become a disciple of Christ.

When we were about start our church I sat down with my long-time pastor, Tom Peters. As we sat in my office, he began to share from his wealth of knowledge on pastoring. He and his wife did an incredible job over the years. They came from North Florida to a dry church with only 8 members. Their first prayer meeting was a total washout. But they put their hand to the plow and never looked back. Over his 40 years of ministry, pastor Tom spent his energy studying and preaching, building facilities, counseling people, leading a staff of men and women, raising millions of dollars for missionaries all over the world, and much, much more. At the end of his tenure, they saw those 8 people in that dilapidated prayer room grow to over 2,000 people with 7 buildings on 33 acres of land—all paid off! As we finished our nearly 2-hour meeting he said, "Oh and Dan, one more thing… As I look at my hands and feet, I can see that I'm much older now, and I can't do the things that I used to do. Time goes so fast. So, Dan, make your time count. Make your time count for God. Because there will come a day when you won't be able to do the things you used to do."

My charge to you is the same. Before you know it you won't be able to do the things you can do now. Give God all you have and live for Him completely. Do it before it's too late. Do it and do it now! For you are here for a limited time only.

Psalm 39:4-7 (NLT)

"Lord, remind me how brief my time on earth will be. Remind me that my days are numbered- how fleeting my life is. You have made my life no longer than the width of my hand. My entire lifetime is just a moment to you; at best, each of us is but a breath. We are merely moving shadows, and all our busy rushing ends in nothing. We heap up wealth, not knowing who will spend it. And so, Lord, where do I put my hope? My only hope is in you."

My Dad's Cabin
Discover your gifts, and then use them to bless others
– for the glory of God!

www.ingramcontent.com/pod-product-compliance
Lightning Source LLC
Chambersburg PA
CBHW060036050426
42448CB00012B/3030